the LAST YEARS of the

CLASS 40s

A. WYN HOBSON

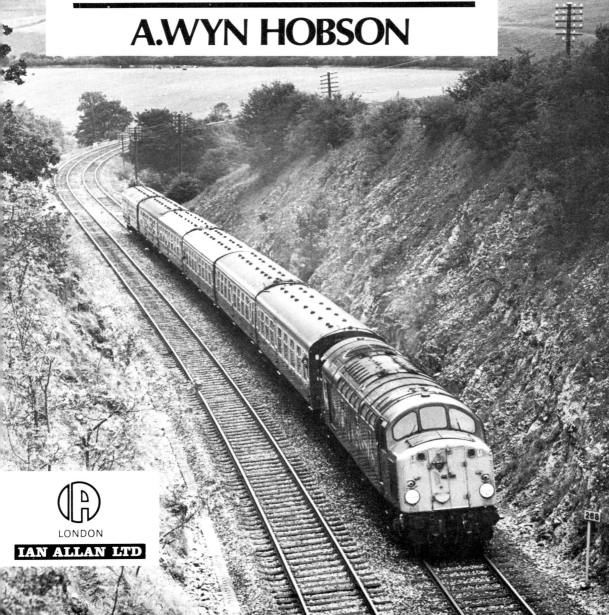

LONDON
IAN ALLAN LTD

Front cover: Class 40 No 40.188 at Berwick on
3 August 1981 with an up Freightliner.
L. A. Nixon

Back cover: No 40.188 passes Newton-le-
Willows, Lancashire, with an eastbound coal train
on 3 March 1976. *David A. Flitcroft*

Previous page: No 40.004 climbs past Smardale
with the 16.35 Carlisle-Leeds, in September
1983. *Les Nixon*

First published 1985

ISBN 0 7110 1467 1

© Ian Allan Ltd 1985

Published by Ian Allan Ltd, Shepperton, Surrey; and printed
by Ian Allan Printing Ltd at their works at Coombelands in
Runnymede, England.

Introduction

The most potent memories will be of their
sounds: and for each of us who knew them, there
will be particular recollections.

For me, one such begins with the warm
stillness of summer nights, at the top of a house
in Caernarfon in the late 1960s and mid-1970s.
Outside, and below on the gradually falling slope
with its geometric outcrops of houses and
gardens, the unvarying light of sodium lamps on
the deserted A487 road. Somewhere in the
darkness of the seashore beyond, the tentative,
questing note of a lone oyster-catcher. The low,
breathy onrush of an isolated passing car blots
out the bird's thin call for a few moments, before
fading away into the distance, leaving once more
only the leisurely lapping of water on the beach,
and the sporadic, absorbed signals of a pair of
scavenging gulls.

And then, away to the northwest, across the
Menai Straits and the darkened landmass of
Anglesey, a distant throbbing hum suddenly rises
out of the stillness. A Class '40' on the up 'Irish
Mail'; the sound, now obscured by the
configurations of rolling fields, now clearer
again, slowly gaining in strength as the train
sweeps along the rising gradients past Llangaffo,
miles away across land and water; and then
fading into inaudibility as it continues eastward,
towards Bangor, Crewe, London.

Minutes of stillness and nightbirds. Then, to
the northeast, the sound of the down train.
Another '40' – the deep throb more insistent as
the locomotive pounds past Gaerwen,
accelerating its train from the permanent way
slack over the Britannia Bridge; a pulsing rumble
and faraway muffled roar of wheels on steel rail,
in distant brooding counterpoint to the slow, high
trills of the oyster-catcher on the beach below.
The train never visible; the beat of the engine
moving steadily across the invisible landscape
and away across Malltraeth Marsh; and the sound
of the train slowly fading, until it disappears in
the deep, scarcely audible whisper of the night
world.

Another memory (again, not of one occasion
but of many) begins at another open window, this
time of a door or compartment in a Mark I coach,
at the front of a down train standing in
Penmaenmawr station. A '40' at the head; at this
close range, the rhythmic elements of the
engine's quiet, idling rumble are more clearly
audible, and above it the warbling whistle that
was so characteristic of this class. The right-away
is given: the rumble and the whistle rise in pitch

and accelerate, in a brief series of surges, as the power-handle is opened up and the train moves away purposefully. Almost immediately it meets the short sharp climb, under a bridge and up through a shallow cutting past the granite works, on a gradient of 1 in 132; the rumble of the engine is now a loud urgent pulsating, sharpened at its higher levels into throaty staccato chatter, the whistle a relentless sibilant shrilling above it. The locomotive breasts the summit of the climb, but there is no slackening, and it bores onward at full throttle under two stone bridges, past a derelict granite works, round the curve of the cliff edge and into Penclip Tunnel, where the rumble explodes into a thunderous throbbing musical roar, echoing in the wide twilit spaces of the avalanche-shelter and drowning out all other sound and sensation, as the train rushes headlong onward into the darkness of the central tunnel itself.

Other memories are of single experiences. A 40's' engine opening up to a tremendous assault of sound as it accelerates a heavy down relief from a near-stand at signals just short of Llandudno Junction station one summer day in the mid-1960s; locomotive and train leaning to the curve through the platforms, and the racing roar of the engine a strange contrast with the locomotive's slow advance. And another summer day, this time in 1981. My attention is concentrated on my feet, as I negotiate the peaty, tussocky ground of the descending slopes below the summit of Bera Mawr. Sun and diaphanous cloud patches above; my parents and a family friend a few yards ahead. Somewhere below us to the right, invisible and inaudible, lie Aber Falls. To the left, the long bleak hump of Moel Wnion stretches away towards the west. Ahead and beyond, in a tiny gap made by the steep little valley above Aber village, a glimpse of Lavan Sands, the sea, and Penmon Point far beyond.

I pause in momentary disbelief at the sudden sound of a train engine. The village of Llanfairfechan, four miles away and nearly 2,000ft below, is hidden from our view by foothills, but the direction and character of the sound make it clear that what I can hear is a train leaving the station; the locomotive, unmistakably, a '40'; the sound astonishingly clear.

As on those nights years before, I track the train's progress by its sound. I watch the gap between the steep distant slopes, and try to identify the line of the railway among the few green and golden fields I can see beyond. At length, moving along a black strip that I have mistaken for hedgerows, a just-identifiable but familiar twin-nosed silhouette appears – unbelievably tiny, considering the volume of sound it has thrown up into the hills. Locomotive

and train thread across the gap and are lost to sight; but for some minutes afterwards, their waning sound intermittently drifts over the rim of Moel Wnion, as the train heads through the distant woods towards Bangor.

And the earliest recollections. October 1960, Euston – the old Euston, before rebuilding. My first-ever visit to London; and, after a first trainspotting summer in which I had seen just two 'English Electric Type 4s' (as the Class 40s were known then) on my home territory, and had had to content myself with scrutinising photographs of others in the pages of *Trains Illustrated*, there were suddenly numerous Type 4s to be seen. New ones, mostly – the green paint still bright. Almost every lunchtime for a week, we repaired to the Euston buffet, and I made a tour of the arrival platforms to see what 'Princess' or 'Coronation' Pacific had arrived; and Type 4s fresh from Vulcan Foundry. D294, D295, D297, D298, D299 – would D300 arrive by the end of the week? That did not transpire. But in that week I came to know intimately the explosive deep-throated rattle of a '40's' engine being started up from rest, and the upward rising of the whistling sound that would become so familiar over the next 25 years.

There will be some who read this book – especially in years to come – who will never have known the Class '40s', and know virtually nothing about them. As a starting point for some further introduction to these locomotives, I need move only a few yards, to one of the lesser arrival platforms at that same Euston station, where, every lunchtime during that autumn week in 1960, I saw another diesel locomotive arriving unobtrusively with what was evidently a semi-fast service from somewhere; one or other of two older diesels, numbered 10201 and 10203. Memory is inevitably unreliable at this distance in time but my recollection suggests that these machines were in every way quieter, when idling at least, than the Type 4s whose engines and peremptory horns so commanded attention a few yards away. There was nothing about these other, older locomotives to suggest, to my young mind, any kind of mechanical family connection. Yet they, along with No 10202 which was still operating somewhere on the Southern Region, were in most important respects the immediate precursors of the Class '40s'.

The Southern Railway, as it then was, had originally announced its intention of experimenting with main line diesel traction in 1946. However, it was the LMS which produced the first main line diesel locomotive for use in the British Isles: No 10000, which emerged from Derby Works at the end of 1947, a few weeks before the nationalisation of the railways. Its sister engine. No 10001, appeared a few weeks later. Perhaps their main visible contribution to the development of Class '40', and certain other locomotive classes of the late 1950s and early 1960s, was the use of two nose ends, at the extremities of the bodywork. These were functional in that they housed some essential mechanical equipment, but were also very much influenced by contemporary American design practice.

The engine for this locomotive design was provided by the English Electric Co, which had amassed considerable experience of building main line diesels for export in the foregoing years. It was a 16-cylinder machine, in which two banks of eight cylinders were arranged into a V-formation, and developed 1,600 brake horsepower at an engine-speed of 750rpm. The electric current it generated was fed to traction motors mounted on the axles of the locomotive's six-wheel bogies. Such was the diesel engine's success in service that it was used in the first two of the Southern Region's diesels, Nos 10201 and 10202, which at last appeared at the end of 1950.

Externally, these locomotives were quite different from their LMS cousins. No projecting noses were employed, and in design the locomotives were virtually box-shaped, with slightly rounded contours. Their bogies, designed by O. V. S. Bulleid, the last Chief Mechanical Engineer of the Southern Railway and the designer of the 'Merchant Navy' and 'West Country' Pacifics, were longer than those of 10000/1, and contained eight wheels as against the LMS bogies' six. The additional axle was unpowered, and pivoted in a pony-truck assembly within the bogie; its primary purpose was to spread the weight of the locomotive, in order to reduce wear on the SR track and remain within the axle-loading restrictions obtaining on that Region. The bogies were plateframed, and the locomotive buffers and drawgear were mounted directly on them. When the Class '40s' came to be designed, it was decided to incorporate this bogie design in them, largely unaltered beyond a change in wheel-diameter; by that time, civil engineers' departments on other Regions had become, for the time being, wary in the matter of axle loadings on main line diesel locomotives.

The two new SR machines were tried out in service for some years, but their performance was not spectacular, partly because so much of the power generated by the engine was being used up simply in moving the locomotive's 135 tons weight. In 1954, an improved version appeared, in the shape of No 10203. This locomotive had a slightly reduced weight of just over 132 tons, and the engine was a more powerful development of the English Electric 16SVT engine used in its predecessors, and developed 2,000bhp at a speed of 850rpm. No 10203 proved the most successful in service of the five pioneering main line locomotives, and the new engine, like the bogies, was eventually incorporated in the Class '40' design.

In 1955, the Modernisation Plan for British Railways appeared, decreeing the end of steam traction. An early stage in the Plan's implementation involved a 'Pilot Scheme' in which various manufacturers were invited to provide prototype main line diesel locomotives for evaluation in service. Five type classifications based on engine horsepower were drawn up, and the locomotives that were later to become known as Class 40 fell within the Type 4 category. Ten of these locomotives were ordered from English Electric in 1955, and the first, No D200 (the first high-horsepower mainline diesel locomotive to enter service as a result of the 1955 Plan), emerged from English Electric's Vulcan Foundry, at Newton-le-Willows in Lancashire, in March 1958. The deterioration in British Railways' financial position, in the meantime, brought about the abandonment of the Pilot Scheme before the 10 prototype locomotives had been fully evaluated, and series production soon followed, ending in September 1962 with the appearance of the 200th English Electric Type 4, No D399. One hundred and eighty of the locomotives were built at Vulcan, and the other 20 (originally Nos D305-D324) were built at the former Robert Stephenson & Hawthorns workshops at Darlington, while construction of the production 'Deltic' (Class 55) locomotives was being started at Vulcan.

The internal mechanical and electrical arrangements of the Class '40s' have been exhaustively discussed elsewhere, and thus, in what is primarily a pictorial volume on the class, it is appropriate to concentrate henceforward on the visible external features and variants of the class's design. The external variants were, in fact, to be more numerous than on most British main line diesel classes.

The use of nose ends was common to the whole class, and the design of the nose and cab window assembly is generally agreed to have been more elegant than on Nos 10000/1. However, considerable alterations in detail to the nose ends occurred both during series production and in later years. Locomotive D200 to D344 were built with gangway doors in the centre of each nose end. These were provided in order that crews could move between locomotives in the event of double-headed working (an expedient that had often been resorted to in the early days of the underpowered 10000/1 and 10201/2). These doors were in practice rarely used, however, and a number were in due course sealed up, to reduce the problem of draughts in the driving cabs. In a few Scottish-based examples (D260-D266), the doors were removed altogether in 1965 and replaced by central four-character headcode panels.

Headcode display on the locomotives was itself the subject of variation during series production. Nos D200-D324 were built with a system of four disc-shaped white markers on each nose end, used in various combinations to indicate the type of train being worked (anything from express passenger to local goods or a locomotive running light), on a pattern similar to the headlamp combinations used on steam locomotives for the same purpose. The discs were hinged, and could be folded out of use; when in use, they exposed white lights through holes in the lower halves, for night-time identification. In later years, the discs were removed from some locomotives, leaving only the marker lights.

During 1960, British Railways decided on a new policy with regard to train headcodes. With the partial exception of Southern Region workings, trains were now to be described by means of a four-character code: a single number, indicating the type of train being worked; a letter, indicating destination area; and two numbers which were the reporting number of the individual train. Locomotives D325-D344 were built with two headcode display boxes on each nose end, placed on either side of the gangway doors. The two tail lights (placed just under half way up the sides of the nose end on locomotives D200-D324) were moved down to occupy the position formerly occupied by the outer marker discs. The headcode boxes each displayed two of the headcode characters, which were printed in white on a black background on fabric rolls, and illuminated from behind at night.

The final batch of Class '40s', D345-D399, were built without gangway doors, and the headcode display was now in a single four-character headcode display box mounted just above the centre of the nose end. In contrast to the sharp right-angled corners of the headcode boxes in the later Scottish conversions, these headcode boxes had slightly rounded corners; and as with the previous variant in headcode display arrangements, there were some attendant alterations in the positioning of nose end handrails and lamp brackets.

In January 1976, British Rail (as it had by now become) decided to dispense with headcode displays on locomotives. For a time, locomotives ran with the roller blinds wound to display four zeros, but in due course various substitutes for these blinds were devised. The one used on Class '40' was to insert black adhesive panels behind the glass of the headcode box or boxes, leaving a total of two translucent white circles on each nose end headcode display, illuminated from behind at night.

In later years, a few further variations occurred on certain locomotives, generally as a result of collision damage repairs, or substitution of parts during major works overhauls. One example was the appearance of a twin-headcode-box locomotive with gangway doors from one of the earlier batch of locomotives, still carrying two marker discs. Most of the variants in headcode display arrangements that were still visible in the period covered by this book are illustrated in the following pages.

Upon entry into service, the Class '40s' were allocated to depots on the Eastern, London Midland, Scottish and North Eastern Regions of British Railways. During the 1970s, most of the class was gradually concentrated on the London Midland Region, with the remainder allocated to the ER in Yorkshire and on Teesside; but they continued to operate services over a wide area of the British Rail system, as is illustrated in this book. Twenty-five locomotives (D210-D225 and D227-D235) of the first batch to be allocated to the LMR from 1959 were, between 1960 and 1963, given the names of famous ocean liners associated with the Port of Liverpool during previous decades. Each nameplate, cast in metal, consisted of a narrow horizontal rectangle bearing the name of a ship, and the name of the owning steamship company in smaller lettering below it. The whole was surmounted by a roughly seven-eighths segment of a circle, containing the badge of the steamship company painted within a ship's steering-wheel motif. Lettering, motif and rims were in raised relief on a red background.

A BR policy decision in 1970 led to the gradual removal of these nameplates, some being disposed of by sale, some being stolen and a few being retained for use on special occasions. For a while only a group of bolts in the bodyside marked the former position of each nameplate; however, in due course the names formerly carried were painted on the sides of most of the locomotives, in these positions. Some were stencilled on in white paint and in other cases the letters were hand-painted. Later, attempts to reproduce the rectangular shape of the original nameplate (albeit without the steamship company name or the badge/motif) were made on a few locomotives, with a rectangular rim, painted in white, framing white-painted lettering on a red or light blue background. In 1980, there was also a brief spate of unofficial namings, perpetrated by enthusiastic BR depot staff and swiftly vetoed by higher authority. Known examples of these applications of unofficial names were *Warrior* to 40.104 (as No D304 had by then become), *Spartan* to 40.131, *Hurricane* to 40.132, *Andromeda* to 40.134, *Trojan* to 40.137, *Panther* to 40.145, and *Lismore* to 40.164. For a few days, No 40.129 even sported the name *Dracula!*

The Class '40s', when built, were painted in British Railways standard green, with grey roof and a light grey shoulder band at the top of each bodyside, below the roof-mounted filter louvres. The British Railways totem symbol was applied on each side above the No 2 bogie, and the numbers were applied beneath the four cabside windows in block-style numerals and lettering. The first of many variations in livery style came when a rectangular area on the lower half of each nose end was painted yellow, from 1962 onwards, in line with a general BR policy to improve the visibility of locomotives to trackside workers and others. In 1967, the decision was taken to increase the size of the yellow-painted area at the ends of all types of locomotives, and in the case of the Class '40s' this led to the repainting of the whole nose end in yellow, with a slight wrap-around onto the top and sides of the nose.

From 1968, the new BR blue livery began to be applied to the remainder of the body superstructure of the Class '40s'. The new British Rail 'reversed arrow' logo was applied in the positions formerly occupied by the locomotive numbers, the latter being moved to a position behind the cab doors and in line with the logos. A more rounded style of numerals was adopted for numbers, and after the withdrawal of BR's last steam locomotives in 1968, the 'D' prefix on BR diesel locomotives was discontinued. It was also at this time that the 'English Electric Type 4s' were officially designated Class 40.

Then, in 1973-74, the whole BR locomotive fleet was renumbered, in order to be compatible with the new computerised TOPS (Total Operations Processing System) for traffic supervision. The new numbers began with the identifying number of the class, followed by a three-figure number for each individual locomotive of the class. In the case of Class '40', the new numbers maintained a degree of numerical continuity with the old ones: thus D201-D321 became 40.001-40.121, and D323-D399 became 40.123-40.199. D200 was renumbered 40.122, filling a gap left by the withdrawal of No D322 from service in December 1967, following a disastrous accident near Warrington in May 1966. As renumbering took place, the number of positions where numbers and logos were applied was reduced, in

each case from four to two, with the logos (latterly of reduced size) being carried under the left-hand cabside windows, and the number behind the left-hand door of each cab.

With the occurrence of so many overlapping changes to elements of the locomotive liveries, it was not surprising that a variety of combinations of these elements was observed on Class '40s' between the late 1960s and the mid-1970s. The last Class '40' to fall due for repainting from green to blue livery was No 40.106, in 1978; however, the LMR's Chief Mechanical Engineer decided that the locomotive should be repainted in green, with British Railways totems, so that it could be used for railtour and other special work when required. The grey bodyside shoulder band was not retained, however, and the nose ends had to remain all yellow. When the engine of No 40.106 became unserviceable in 1983, necessitating its withdrawal from service in April, BR were prevailed upon (partly by representations from the Class 40 Preservation Society) to refurbish No 40.122, then lying out of use at Toton depot, and repaint it in BR green for further service. The British Railways totem was once again applied, replacing the BR reversed arrow logo, and this time the grey shoulder band was also reapplied. The number D200, in the old block style numerals and lettering, was applied beneath both left-hand cabside windows; but the requirements of TOPS made it necessary to apply the number 40.122 beneath both right-hand cabside windows, and the all-yellow nose end had once again to be retained.

A few other alterations to the external appearance of some Class '40s' are worthy of note. In the late 1960s, a general policy decision was made to effect a gradual changeover from vacuum to air-braking in all BR rolling stock, and in the ensuing years a majority of the Class '40s' had additional equipment installed to enable them to work trains of air-braked as well as of vacuum-braked stock. Externally, this involved the installation of additional flexible pipe connections on the bogie headstocks, adjacent to the buffers and drawgear. Another small variation in appearance stemmed from the need to instal a new type of bogie traction motor in the class during the 1960s and 1970s. Until replacement was complete, locomotives which had been so modified had a light blue line painted beneath the locomotive numbers, to distinguish them from unmodified machines.

From 1970, the honeycomb pattern grilles across the radiator air intake panels above the No 1 bogie were removed from Eastern Region Class '40s', in order to improve engine cooling by increasing the airflow across the radiator elements. The Scottish Region's Class '40' fleet were similarly adapted soon afterwards, but the London Midland Region authorities remained unwilling to implement this modification for some years, and when transfer of Class '40s' to the LMR from the ER and ScR began, grilles were actually restored in some cases. However, from 1979 the LMR reversed its previous policy, and a gradual removal of all grilles was implemented.

In 1977, the train heating boilers of a large number of Class '40s' were isolated, as by that time there was little solely steam heated passenger stock remaining in service, and relatively few passenger train workings were rostered for Class '40s'. From 1979, the water tanks underslung from the main frames between the bogies, to supply the boiler, were removed from a few Class '40s', leaving only the support brackets visible in the gap.

Up to the end of 1975, only one Class '40', apart from D322, was withdrawn from service: No 40.189, also as a result of collision damage. However, in January 1976 the decision was taken to embark on the phasing out of the class. BR was suffering a general recession in freight and parcels traffic, and maintenance and reliability problems with the class had shown some tendency to grow rather than diminish with the passage of years. However, when it is recalled that the life expectancy of main line diesel locomotive classes on BR averages some 15 years, the fact that the oldest Class '40s' had put in 18 years' service before phasing-out was decided upon is, on the face of it, surprising; and the fact that, at the beginning of 1984, some 50 of the class were still in service, including some of the original batch of 10, now nearly 26 years old, marks out Class '40' as having been remarkable among British main line diesels.

Why did Class '40' achieve such a long service record without major mechanical modification? There were, after all, a number of reasons for expecting the reverse. By the standards of what in due course proved to be technically feasible, the '40s', at 133 tons (134 tons when air-brake equipment was added) were considerably overweight in relation to the power of their engines. Their powers of acceleration were only moderate, and their top speed of 90mph was soon insufficient to meet the requirements of front-rank express passenger train operation. As a class, they were more than usually vulnerable to varying standards of maintenance as between depot and depot, and the electrical equipment, though robust and reliable, was slightly less efficient in transmitting power than that of later locomotive classes. The long bogies, too, were always troublesome: the unpowered pony truck had a slight tendency to derail when working over uneven track in yards and industrial exchange sidings or over exceptionally complex pointwork; and, lacking secondary suspension, the bogies were also hard-riding, and set up considerable stresses both on the track and in their own drawgear.

And yet the locomotives continued to be retained for service by BR management. Indeed, the withdrawal programme was slowed down in 1978, following an upsurge in freight traffic, and its resumption, still at a relatively moderate pace, from late 1980 was accompanied at one stage by rumours, strong enough to be quoted in parts of the railway press, that management was considering a plan to refurbish selected members of the class and put them to work on freight in the South Wales valleys. In the event, nothing came of this idea; but the fact that it could be seriously entertained, 20-odd years after the locomotives' first appearance, is noteworthy. What qualities did the Class '40s' possess that led to their longevity, and to their having been, as has been remarked, 'everybody's favourite standby'?

The point was, perhaps, that the equipment of which the Class '40s' were constructed was robust and, with the occasional exception of the bogies and a few smaller components, very reliable. Moreover, the load-spreading characteristics of the bogies gave the locomotives a wide route availability, which led to their being seen on nearly all the primary and secondary rail routes of Britain at one time or another. Two reasons for the general robustness of the design can be adduced. Firstly, the locomotives were very solidly constructed (to the extent of being quite difficult and expensive to reduce to scrap upon withdrawal!), and secondly, the design of the engine, in particular, was one in which the power output was well within the physical tolerances of the unit producing it. The English Electric engine, with its 16 cylinders, suffered few problems of engine stress; by contrast, the three versions of the Sulzer 12LDA28 engine used in various BR Type 4 designs (later known as Classes '44' to '47') were far more prone to such problems, as an output of anything from 2,300bhp to 2,700bhp was being demanded from a power unit of only 12 cylinders. Indeed, the 12LDA28-C installed in the Class '47' design eventually had to be derated by over 100hp, as a result of numerous problems in service – an expedient that has never been resorted to on an English Electric diesel locomotive engine.

The difference in design philosophy between the two engines was also, incidentally, responsible for the differences between their characteristic sounds. The deep rumble of the Class '40s' resulted from the use of an engine and cylinders that were physically relatively large;

the Sulzer engine was more compact and had smaller cylinders, which were nonetheless required to do a larger amount of work, and thus produced a thinner, faster sound. (The distinctive whistling noise on the Class '40s', which led to their becoming affectionately known as the 'Whistlers' among the enthusiast fraternity, was caused by the physical design characteristics of the single-stage turbines through which exhaust gases flowed to operate the engine's turbochargers.)

Another factor making for the longevity of the Class '40s' was probably the ready availability of a number of the necessary spare parts, as these were interchangeable with those of more recent English Electric-built and English Electric-engined locomotives on BR. Lastly, even though the Class '40s' were soon found to be inadequate for the front rank passenger duties for which they had been intended, they were more than equal to the demands of the secondary passenger and parcels services to which they were transferred, and their generous physical tolerances gave them a capacity for being worked hard for long periods that made them very suitable indeed for heavy freight work.

In respect of passenger train operation, there were certain secondary routes with which the Class '40s' became particularly associated. They dominated the Edinburgh-Aberdeen (and later some Glasgow-Aberdeen) services for many years before their transfer south; and having made an appearance on some North Wales Coast workings from the early 1960s, they worked most locomotive-hauled passenger services on that line between the end of steam working, in January 1967, and May 1979, only gradually giving way to Class '47s' and Class '45s'. They were also staple motive power on services between Liverpool and Newcastle from the early 1960s to the mid-1970s, and a relatively brief spell of work on Settle and Carlisle route passenger services in the late 1970s and early 1980s coincided with widespread interest in that route, pending its closure as a through line, and helped to keep the '40s' at the centre of enthusiasts' attention. They were also employed extensively on summer Saturday inter-Regional workings to holiday resorts such as Llandudno, Blackpool and Skegness, and their rostering for some of these workings lasted into the 1980s.

On freight work, the '40s' were even more widely travelled, though most of their work was concentrated in the north of England. They were also much used on special workings such as engineers' ballast and breakdown trains, and for haulage of Inter-City trains complete with 'dead' electric locomotives when engineering works necessitated the switching-off of current on the electrified West Coast main line.

The photographs in this volume depict Class '40s' in operation after January 1976, when the phasing-out of the class was announced. I have, in compiling this selection, aimed to provide a wide-ranging pictorial impression of the Class '40s' at work and at rest during their last years, rather than a precise record of all their workings, regular and exceptional; and in this I hope for the indulgence of any reader who, remembering the period, may feel that a particular area or train-working has (quite accidentally) received greater, or less, representation than some others, in these pages. At all events, this book reflects something of the great variety of locations in which Class '40s' could be seen, especially on freight workings, during their last years, and I hope that those who loved and admired the sight and the sounds of them will find it a fitting memorial.

A. Wyn Hobson

Class 40–a select Locomotive history

Original BR No	BR TOPS No	Date to traffic	Original allocation (Region)	Date of withdrawal
D200	40.122	3/1958	E	9/1981*
D201	40.001	4/1958	E	7/1984
D202	40.002	4/1958	E	5/1984
D203	40.003	5/1958	E	9/1982
D204	40.004	5/1958	E	9/1984
D205	40.005	6/1958	E	1/1976
D206	40.006	7/1958	E	3/1983
D207	40.007	7/1958	E	2/1983
D208	40.008	8/1958	E	11/1982
D209	40.009	9/1958	E	11/1984
D210	40.010	5/1959	LM	9/1981
D211	40.011	6/1959	LM	10/1980
D212	40.012	6/1959	LM	
D213	40.013	6/1959	LM	1/1985
D214	40.014	6/1959	LM	11/1981
D215	40.015	7/1959	LM	11/1984
D216	40.016	7/1959	LM	5/1981
D217	40.017	7/1959	LM	2/1981
D218	40.018	7/1959	LM	9/1981
D219	40.019	7/1959	LM	12/1981
D220	40.020	8/1959	LM	8/1982
D221	40.021	8/1959	LM	7/1976
D222	40.022	8/1959	LM	3/1984
D223	40.023	8/1959	LM	5/1981
D224	40.024	9/1959	LM	6/1984

Original BR No	BR TOPS No	Date to traffic	Original allocation (Region)	Date of withdrawal	Original BR No	BR TOPS No	Date to traffic	Original allocation (Region)	Date of withdrawal
D225	40.025	9/1959	LM	10/1982	D286	40.086	7/1960	NE	1/1985
D226	40.026	9/1959	LM	8/1980	D287	40.087	8/1960	LM	8/1982
D227	40.027	9/1959	LM	4/1983	D288	40.088	8/1960	LM	2/1982
D228	40.028	9/1959	LM	10/1984	D289	40.089	9/1960	LM	7/1976
D229	40.029	9/1959	LM	4/1984	D290	40.090	9/1960	LM	11/1983
D230	40.030	10/1959	LM	4/1983	D291	40.091	9/1960	LM	9/1984
D231	40.031	10/1959	LM	5/1981	D292	40.092	9/1960	LM	11/1982
D232	40.032	10/1959	LM	2/1981	D293	40.093	10/1960	LM	12/1983
D233	40.033	10/1959	LM	9/1984	D294	40.094	10/1960	LM	10/1982
D234	40.034	10/1959	LM	1/1984	D295	40.095	10/1960	LM	9/1981
D235	40.035	10/1959	LM	9/1984	D296	40.096	10/1960	LM	12/1983
D236	40.036	11/1959	LM	1/1982	D297	40.097	11/1960	LM	6/1983
D237	40.037	10/1959	NE	8/1981	D298	40.098	11/1960	LM	4/1981
D238	40.038	10/1959	NE	12/1980	D299	40.099	11/1960	LM	10/1984
D239	40.039	10/1959	NE	1/1976	D300	40.100	11/1960	LM	12/1980
D240	40.040	10/1959	NE	7/1980	D301	40.101	11/1960	LM	8/1982
D241	40.041	10/1959	NE	7/1976	D302	40.102	12/1960	LM	1/1976
D242	40.042	11/1959	NE	12/1980	D303	40.103	12/1960	LM	2/1982
D243	40.043	11/1959	NE	1/1976	D304	40.104	12/1960	LM	1/1985
D244	40.044	11/1959	NE	1/1985	D305	40.105	10/1960	LM	12/1980
D245	40.045	11/1959	NE	8/1976	D306	40.106	11/1960	LM	4/1983
D246	40.046	11/1959	NE	2/1983	D307	40.107	11/1960	LM	12/1981
D247	40.047	11/1959	NE	11/1984	D308	40.108	12/1960	LM	8/1980
D248	40.048	11/1959	NE	10/1977	D309	40.109	12/1960	LM	12/1980
D249	40.049	11/1959	NE	1/1983	D310	40.110	12/1960	LM	12/1980
D250	40.050	12/1959	NE	8/1983	D311	40.111	12/1960	LM	5/1981
D251	40.051	12/1959	NE	1/1978	D312	40.112	12/1960	LM	12/1980
D252	40.052	12/1959	NE	6/1983	D313	40.113	12/1960	LM	10/1981
D253	40.053	1/1960	NE	8/1976	D314	40.114	12/1960	LM	12/1980
D254	40.054	12/1959	NE	12/1977	D315	40.115	1/1961	LM	3/1982
D255	40.055	1/1960	LM	11/1982	D316	40.116	1/1961	LM	2/1981
D256	40.056	1/1960	NE	9/1984	D317	40.117	2/1961	LM	9/1981
D257	40.057	2/1960	NE	7/1984	D318	40.118	2/1961	LM	
D258	40.058	2/1960	NE	9/1984	D319	40.119	3/1961	LM	12/1980
D259	40.059	2/1960	Sc	8/1977	D320	40.120	3/1961	LM	5/1981
D260	40.060	2/1960	Sc	1/1985	D321	40.121	4/1961	LM	3/1983
D261	40.061	2/1960	Sc	6/1983	D322	–	4/1961	LM	12/1967
D262	40.062	9/1960	Sc	11/1981	D323	40.123	5/1961	LM	7/1980
D263	40.063	3/1960	Sc	4/1984	D324	40.124	7/1961	LM	1/1984
D264	40.064	3/1960	Sc	4/1982	D325	40.125	12/1960	LM	5/1981
D265	40.065	3/1960	Sc	11/1981	D326	40.126	12/1960	LM	2/1984
D266	40.066	3/1960	Sc	4/1981	D327	40.127	12/1960	LM	2/1982
D267	40.067	3/1960	LM	7/1981	D328	40.128	1/1961	LM	9/1982
D268	40.068	4/1960	NE	7/1983	D329	40.129	1/1961	LM	5/1984
D269	40.069	4/1960	LM	9/1983	D330	40.130	2/1961	LM	3/1982
D270	40.070	4/1960	NE	6/1981	D331	40.131	2/1961	LM	10/1983
D271	40.071	4/1960	NE	12/1980	D332	40.132	2/1961	LM	3/1982
D272	40.072	4/1960	NE	8/1977	D333	40.133	2/1961	LM	1/1984
D273	40.073	5/1980	NE	6/1983	D334	40.134	3/1961	LM	5/1981
D274	40.074	5/1960	NE	3/1984	D335	40.135	3/1961	LM	1/1985
D275	40.075	5/1960	NE	12/1981	D336	40.136	3/1961	LM	5/1982
D276	40.076	5/1960	NE	4/1983	D337	40.137	3/1961	LM	1/1981
D277	40.077	5/1960	NE	6/1983	D338	40.138	4/1961	LM	8/1982
D278	40.078	6/1960	NE	8/1981	D339	40.139	4/1961	LM	2/1982
D279	40.079	6/1960	NE	1/1985	D340	40.140	4/1961	LM	3/1982
D280	40.080	6/1960	NE	9/1983	D341	40.141	5/1961	LM	9/1983
D281	40.081	6/1960	NE	2/1983	D342	40.142	5/1961	LM	4/1980
D282	40.082	6/1960	NE	11/1984	D343	40.143	5/1961	LM	1/1985
D283	40.083	7/1960	NE	11/1981	D344	40.144	5/1961	LM	5/1981
D284	40.084	7/1960	NE	5/1983	D345	40.145	5/1961	NE	6/1983
D285	40.085	7/1960	NE	3/1984	D346	40.146	5/1961	NE	12/1980

Original BR No	BR TOPS No	Date to traffic	Original allocation (Region)	Date of withdrawal
D347	40.147	5/1961	NE	9/1980
D348	40.148	6/1961	NE	8/1982
D349	40.149	6/1961	NE	8/1981
D350	40.150	6/1961	NE	1/1985
D351	40.151	6/1961	NE	2/1981
D352	40.152	7/1961	NE	1/1985
D353	40.153	7/1961	NE	10/1983
D354	40.154	7/1961	NE	1/1982
D355	40.155	8/1961	NE	1/1985
D356	40.156	8/1961	NE	7/1980
D357	40.157	9/1961	Sc	7/1983
D358	40.158	9/1961	Sc	12/1983
D359	40.159	10/1961	Sc	3/1982
D360	40.160	10/1961	Sc	11/1984
D361	40.161	10/1961	Sc	12/1980
D362	40.161	11/1961	Sc	12/1982
D363	40.163	11/1961	Sc	6/1982
D364	40.164	11/1961	Sc	7/1983
D365	40.165	11/1961	Sc	7/1981
D366	40.166	12/1961	Sc	2/1982
D367	40.167	12/1961	Sc	2/1984
D368	40.168	12/1961	Sc	12/1984
D369	40.169	12/1961	LM	12/1983
D370	40.170	12/1961	LM	12/1983
D371	40.171	12/1961	LM	12/1981
D372	40.172	1/1962	LM	9/1983
D373	40.173	1/1962	LM	8/1981
D374	40.174	1/1962	LM	5/1984
D375	40.175	2/1962	LM	5/1981
D376	40.176	2/1962	LM	8/1981
D377	40.177	2/1962	LM	6/1984
D378	40.178	2/1962	LM	6/1981
D379	40.179	2/1962	LM	2/1981
D380	40.180	3/1962	LM	5/1983
D381	40.181	3/1962	LM	1/1985
D382	40.182	3/1962	LM	6/1982
D383	40.183	3/1962	LM	5/1983
D384	40.184	4/1962	LM	12/1982
D385	40.185	3/1962	NE	8/1983
D386	40.186	4/1962	NE	12/1982
D387	40.187	4/1962	NE	8/1982
D388	40.188	4/1962	NE	8/1983
D389	40.189	5/1962	NE	1/1976
D390	40.190	5/1962	NE	1/1976
D391	40.191	5/1962	NE	9/1983
D392	40.192	5/1962	NE	1/1985
D393	40.193	6/1962	NE	10/1981
D394	40.194	6/1962	NE	1/1985
D395	40.195	6/1962	NE	6/1984
D396	40.196	7/1962	NE	5/1984
D397	40.197	7/1962	NE	9/1983
D398	40.198	8/1962	NE	1/1983
D399	40.199	9/1962	NE	6/1982

* (40.122 temporarily reinstated, (6/1983)

Original BR No	BR TOPS No	Name	Nameplate fitted
D210	40.010	Empress of Britain	5/1960
D211	40.011	Mauretania	9/1960
D212	40.012	Aureol	9/1960
D213	40.013	Andania	6/1962
D214	40.014	Antonia	5/1961
D215	40.015	Aquitania	5/1962
D216	40.016	Campania	5/1962
D217	40.017	Carinthia	5/1962
D218	40.018	Carmania	7/1961
D219	40.019	Caronia	6/1962
D220	40.020	Franconia	2/1963
D221	40.021	Ivernia	3/1961
D222	40.022	Laconia	10/1962
D223	40.023	Lancastria	5/1961
D224	40.024	Lucania	8/1962
D225	40.025	Lusitania	3/1962
D227	40.027	Parthia	6/1962
D228	40.028	Samaria	9/1962
D229	40.029	Saxonia	3/1963
D230	40.030	Scythia	4/1961
D231	40.031	Sylvania	5/1962
D232	40.032	Empress of Canada	3/1961
D233	40.033	Empress of England	9/1961
D234	40.034	Accra	5/1962
D235	40.035	Apapa	5/1962

Modern Railways, June 1965, carried the report that nameplates bearing the name *Media* (a mistake for *Medea*?) had been cast for use on locomotive No D226. No such plates were ever carried by the locomotive.

In the above lists, the dates given are for the 'period ending' in each case. Withdrawal dates are correct to 1/1985

Builders' Works numbers

D200-D304 Vulcan Foundery Nos D395-D541
D305-D324 Robert Stephenson & Hawthorns Nos 8135-8154
D325-D399 Vulcan Foundry Nos D621-D695

Named Locomotives

Note: this list is of locomotives officially named. For a list of locomotives to which unofficial names were briefly applied during 1980 see the Introduction.

English Electric Works numbers

D200-D209	2367-2376
D210-D239	2666-2695
D240-D249	2715-2724
D250-D304	2772-2826
D305-D314	2725-2734
D315-D324	2850-2859
D325-D399	3071-3145

Above: With a deafening crescendo of sound, No 40.092 accelerates an Edinburgh Millerhill-Tyneside coal-empties train through Berwick-upon-Tweed station, after being held in the up loop for the passage of an express on 15 May 1981. This is one of the locomotives originally built with connecting doors and disc-type headcode displays in the nose ends, though on this locomotive the discs were later removed, leaving only the marker lights beneath. *Antony Guppy*

Left: No 40.171 waits at Platform 3 in Crewe station for clearance to run its train, the 09.23 from Holyhead, to the carriage sidings on 6 June 1981. This is one of the final batch of Class '40s', built with four-character headcode panels; the original roller blinds have been replaced by a black adhesive panel containing two translucent marker areas illuminated by the panel lights. *L. Peter Gater*

Above: No 40.015 (formerly named *Aquitania*) pauses with a coal train in the eastbound loop line at Blackburn station on 26 April 1982, while travellers await a Preston-bound DMU. *John Whitehouse*

Below: No 40.012 (formerly *Aureol*) leaves Aintree station with the 11.07 goods for Edge Hill on 7 July 1983. *Kim Fullbrook*

Above right: No 40.129 sorts a goods train at Cyffordd Llandudno (Llandudno Junction) on 7 May 1983. Conwy Castle is visible in the distance on the left. *A. Wyn Hobson*

Below right: No 40.194 prepares to leave the sidings at Hexham with a train of 'Presflo' cement wagons on 30 March 1978. *David C. Pearce*

Left: Although operation of diesel locomotives over the electrified Manchester-Sheffield via Woodhead route was officially discouraged, due to the absence of air shafts in the three-mile long Woodhead Tunnel, through excursion traffic was usually diesel-worked. Here No 40.044 passes Thurlstone signalbox, west of Penistone, with a Wadsley Bridge-Liverpool soccer excursion in April 1980. This locomotive had had its connecting doors completely removed, following collision damage, but still retained its disc markers. *Roger Kaye*

Below left: No 40.132 speeds through Abergele and Pensarn station, on the North Wales coast, with a Trafford Park-Holyhead Freightliner train on 31 May 1980. *Larry Goddard*

Above: In its declining years, the former Midland Railway's line from Leeds to Carlisle via Settle and Ais Gill was often used as a diversionary route during blockages or engineering work on the electrified West Coast main line. On one such occasion, 2 April 1983, No 40.082, on standby pilot duty, stands in the down loop at Blea Moor signalbox as No 40.074 passes with the 08.14 Perth-Manchester Red Bank vans train. Both locomotives still retain connecting doors and disc markers. *Chris Davis*

Below: No 40.135 pauses outside Appleby North signalbox, on the Settle and Carlisle route, for a crew change on 16 December 1981. *Peter Walton*

Left: For many years, Class '40s' were rostered for certain freight workings between Scotland and East Anglia. Here No 40.047 accelerates the 21.35(SX) Mossend Yard-Harwich Parkeston Quay past Elmswell, between Bury St Edmunds and Ipswich, on 10 December 1981.
John C. Baker

Above: In brilliant but icy weather, a Class '40' passes Ribblehead, on the Settle and Carlisle route, with a Glasgow-Manchester Red Bank empty vans train on 16 January 1977. *Chris Davis*

Below: No 40.003 raises a slipstream of powdery snow as it passes Smardale, also on the Settle and Carlisle route, with a vans train on 22 March 1981. *Peter Walton*

17

Above: No 40.197 climbs Belstead Bank, south of Ipswich, with the 23.35(FSX) Mossend Yard-Harwich Parkeston Quay freight on 22 December 1982. *Michael J. Collins*

Right: No 40.149 in the woods near Snailwell Sidings with the 14.25(SX) Harwich Parkeston Quay-Bathgate freight on 14 April 1981. *John C. Baker*

Below: No 40.183 approaches Ravensthorpe, Yorkshire, with an eastbound freight for Healey Mills Yard on 2 April 1980. *David A. Flitcroft*

Above left: No 40.068 near Saxham and Risby, Suffolk, with the 14.25 Harwich Parkeston Quay-Bathgate freight on 3 July 1978. *John C. Baker*

Above: No 40.143 passes Buxworth, in the Peak District, with the 18.09 Manchester-St Pancras parcels train on 20 June 1983. *Steve Turner*

Left: No 40.080 passes Marykirk, north of Montrose, with the 07.40 Glasgow-Aberdeen express on 13 May 1977. *Tom Heavyside*

Below: No 40.012 (formerly *Aureol*) comes off the Sleaford Avoiding Line at Sleaford North signalbox with the summer Saturday 09.22 Yarmouth-Newcastle on 8 August 1981. In the background a Cravens Class 105 DMU, which has called at Sleaford as the 11.43 Skegness-Nottingham service, awaits a clear road. The avoiding line was closed in November 1982. *Geoff Dowling*

Bottom: Class '40s' were requisitioned to haul many enthusiast railtours during their last years. Here Nos 40.012 (formerly *Aureol*) and 40.081 double-head the 'Anglian Whistler' tour past Whittlesea, between March and Peterborough, en route for the Nene Valley Railway on 1 May 1982. *David C. Pearce*

Above: No 40.115 passes Eccles, Manchester, with an eastbound train of empty ballast-wagons on 31 August 1979. The line branching on the left is a connection to the Manchester Ship Canal railway system. *David A. Flitcroft*

Below: No 40.196 approaches Clifton Junction, near Manchester, with a Barrow-in-Furness-Red Bank Sidings parcels train on 30 October 1983. *Kim Fullbrook*

Above: No 40.117 arrives at Whitemoor Yard, Cambridgeshire, with a freight from the south on 22 April 1981. *Les Nixon*

Above: No 40.106, the only Class '40' to retain green livery throughout the class's last years, heads the Sunday 09.30 Birmingham-Preston past Bloxwich, on the freight-only Walsall-Rugeley line in the West Midlands, on 14 March 1982. The train had been diverted due to engineering works. *John Whitehouse*

Below: No 40.196 passes Miles Platting Junction, Manchester, with a Horwich-Dewsnap Sidings trip-freight on 16 March 1982. *Michael Rhodes*

Above: No 40.035 heads a southbound train of steel rail from Workington through the outskirts of Barrow-in-Furness on the evening of 13 August 1982. This locomotive was formerly named *Apapa*; the name can be seen roughly painted at the former position of the nameplate, and even more roughly at the base of the nose. *Geoff Dowling*

Below: No 40.061, a former Scottish Region example with one of its nose ends rebuilt without connecting doors or headcode panel, approaches the eastern end of Healey Mills Yard with a train of empty hopper-wagons on 2 April 1980. *David A. Flitcroft*

Above: No 40.126 stands outside the former LMS goods warehouse at Bolton on 6 November 1981. *David A. Flitcroft*

Below: No 40.084 approaches Shipley from the Bradford direction with a train of scrap metal on 9 September 1981. *Tom Heavyside*

No 40.085 passes New Mills, in the Peak District, with the summer Saturday 08.04 Manchester Piccadilly-Skegness on 13 August 1983. Enthusiasts travelling on the train have adorned the nose with a headboard designed in the style of the nameplates formerly carried by some members of the class.
Steve Turner

Above: No 40.121 passes Masborough, Rotherham, with a northbound freight in March 1980. *Les Nixon*

Below: No 40.004 passes the site of the closed Stockport Tiviot Dale station, on the former Midland Railway route into Manchester, with a westbound train of BOC tank wagons, on 8 July 1976. The train is entering Tiviot Dale Tunnel, whose collapse a few years later during motorway work necessitated the closure of the line. *Tom Heavyside*

Left: No 40.191 takes the Ellesmere Port line at Helsby, Cheshire, with a train of oil tanks on 25 March 1983. On the right, a hybrid three-car DMU has just arrived on a local passenger service from Hooton.
Geoff Dowling

Above: No 40.027 (formerly *Parthia*) near Mossley, in the Pennines, with the summer Saturday 09.00 York-Llandudno on 28 August 1982.
Geoff Dowling

Right: No 40.091 enters Chester with an eastbound coal train on 2 April 1980, during the period when the approach layout at this point was in course of being remodelled. *Larry Goddard*

Left: Apart from a short period after the introduction of Class '47s' to the LMR in the late 1960s, locomotive-hauled passenger workings on the North Wales coast were dominated by Class '40s' from the mid-1960s until the early 1980s. Here No 40.001 arrives at Penmaenmawr with the 16.52 Holyhead-Manchester Victoria on 22 July 1976. *Kevin Lane*

Below: Class '40s' were much in evidence on cross-country passenger workings during their last years. Here No 40.013 (formerly *Andania*) heads the 09.37 Cleethorpes-Sheffield train through Rotherham station on 9 July 1983. A Plasser & Theurer mobile tamping machine stands in the up local platform. *Colin Marsden*

Left: No 40.108 heads a train of vans away from Oldham in the direction of Manchester on 23 May 1979. *Tom Heavyside*

Below: The Class '40s' were much in evidence on local freight workings in many parts of the country during their last years. Having dropped a few wagons in the yard, No 40.114 is leaving Rhyl with a local goods for Colwyn Bay and Llandudno Junction on 6 March 1978. *Larry Goddard*

Above: No 40.079 heads a summer Saturdays-only Manchester-Skegness train past Brookhouse Colliery, south east of Sheffield, on 17 September 1983. *Les Nixon*

Below: No 40.104 passes the interestingly designed ex-LNWR signalbox at Mostyn, on Deeside, with the 11.47 Bangor-Manchester on 24 July 1982. This train was one of a number of North Wales services which, having been DMU-operated since the mid-1960s, were returned to locomotive haulage during the 1980s. *John Whitehouse*

Below: No 40.183 passes Horton-in-Ribblesdale signalbox, on the Settle and Carlisle route, with the 12.35 Healey Mills-Carlisle freight on 4 May 1982. *Graham Scott-Lowe*

Bottom: No 40.140 heads a train of empty limestone hoppers through Marple station, in the Peak District, on 20 August 1979. *Geoff Pinder*

Above: Class '40s' were
frequently employed for haulage
of ballast trains. Here No 40.129
passes Prestatyn station with an
eastbound train of ballast
hoppers on 5 July 1976. At this
time, conversion of the
locomotive's headcode panels to
display white circles on a black
base had not taken place, and the
panel blinds are turned to the
'four zeros' position. *Kevin Lane*

Left: No 40.090 runs round a
Bayston Hill-Guide Bridge
engineer's train of full ballast
hoppers at Dorrington, south of
Shrewsbury on the North and
West route, on 6 September 1983.
John Chalcraft

Left: No 40.084 waits to leave the Amey Roadstone Company's Loughborough yard with a ballast train for Healey Mills on 27 February 1981.
C. John Tuffs

Below: No 40.126 passes Normanton-on-Soar with the 12.16 Loughborough-Healey Mills ballast train on 8 December 1982.
C. John Tuffs

Far left: No 40.143 passes
Northenden Junction, on the
former Cheshire Lines Committee
Glazebrook-Stockport Edgeley
line, south of Manchester, with
westbound limestone hoppers on
7 October 1983. *Kim Fullbrook*

Above and left: Two views of No
40.122/D200, newly repainted in
green livery, on Settle and Carlisle
route passenger workings near
Kirkby Stephen West during
1983.
Peter Walton

Below: No 40.052 near Gosherton, Lincolnshire, with an excursion from Skipton to Spalding on 8 May 1982. *John C. Baker*

Bottom: Having worked an overnight freight from Mossend Yard to Harwich Parkeston Quay, No 40.004 runs light past North Fen Crossing, near Black Bank, Cambridgeshire, on its way to March depot on 10 September 1983. *John C. Baker*

Right: No 40.030 (formerly *Scythia*) passes Elmswell with the 20.08(SX) Mossend Yard-Harwich Parkeston Quay freight on 18 January 1983. *John C. Baker*

Below right: No 40.036 passes Kearsley power station, near Bolton, with a northbound freight on 4 March 1977. *David A. Flitcroft*

Above: No 40.183 near Aber,
North Wales, with the 09.45
Manchester-Bangor on 29 May
1982. *A. Wyn Hobson*

Right: No 40.129 crosses the fens
near Shippea Hill, East Anglia,
with the summer Saturday 14.34
Yarmouth-Manchester Piccadilly
on 13 July 1983.
Michael J. Collins

Far right: No 40.162 waits in the
down loop at
Berwick-upon-Tweed with a Tyne
Yard-Edinburgh Millerhill coal
train on 15 May 1981.
Antony Guppy

Below: Though Class '40s' were not as frequently seen at work on the southern section of the East Coast main line as on some other major routes, they put in occasional appearances until the very end of the class's operations. In the heat of 27 August 1981, No 40.074 hauls dead Class '55' No 55.007 *Pinza* past Grantham, en route from New England depot, Peterborough, to York for repairs. *Antony Guppy*

Bottom: Reliable as they were, Class '40s' had their share of failures in service. Here No 40.044 awaits a relief locomotive after being declared a failure at Sheffield station while working a Cleethorpes-Manchester parcels train on 9 March 1982. *Bert Wynn*

Above: No 40.070 catches the dying rays of a November sun in 1976, as it awaits a clear road from York with a southbound parcels train. *John Whitehouse*

Below: No 40.022 (formerly *Laconia*) glimpsed at March station on 30 June 1983. *Geoff Pinder*

Above: Still showing four zeros in its headcode panel, No 40.175 rolls a freight out of Dewsnap Sidings, Guide Bridge, on 29 March 1977, passing a collection of Class '25' and Class '47' diesels, and Woodhead route Class '76' electric locomotives. *Chris Davis*

Left: No 40.057 arrives at Glasgow Central station with parcels stock on 28 May 1977. The sparser catenary required for 25kV ac electrification, compared with the 1,500V dc electrification of the 1950s, is well illustrated in the comparison with the Guide Bridge picture, above. *Chris Davis*

Right: Class '40s' were often called upon to assist locomotives which had failed in service. In sub-zero temperatures on 12 December 1981, No 40.068 hammers through Haringay, North London, with failed Class '47/4' No 47.431 and the 08.07 York-Kings Cross in tow. The train was running over two hours late after failure at Yaxley, near Peterborough. *Antony Guppy*

Below: The train-heating boiler of No 40.027 (formerly *Parthia*) blows off as the locomotive awaits departure from Birmingham New Street with the Sunday 14.05 for Manchester Piccadilly on 30 April 1978. Use of diesel locomotives on the central sections of the West Coast main line is frequently resorted to when electric current is switched off for weekend engineering work to take place. *C. John Tuffs*

Above: A cloud of smoke from two of the exhaust ports indicates that all is far from well with the engine of No 40.197 as it approaches Stalybridge with the summer Saturday 08.31 Leeds-Blackpool on 28 August 1982. *John Whitehouse*

Left: No 40.148 slowly accelerates out of a down loop south of York station with a Rotherham-Motherwell steel train on 26 October 1978. *C. John Tuffs*

Above right: No 40.012 (formerly *Aureol*) passes Cheadle with a train of chemical tankers from ICI's Folly Lane Works to Immingham on 15 September 1983. The rivets marking the position of the former nameplate can be clearly seen in this side-lit view, and the name has been painted on the locomotive side in the appropriate position. *Kim Fullbrook*

Right: No 40.157 passes Dringhouses, south of York, with a northbound parcels train on 7 April 1983. *Michael J. Collins*

Above left: No 40.135 passes the remains of Talacre station, on Deeside, with the 13.58 Bangor-Manchester Victoria on 24 July 1982. *John Whitehouse*

Left: No 40.049 passes an interesting two-way semaphore signal gantry at Haltwhistle station, Northumberland, on 8 June 1981, with a mixed freight for Carlisle. The disused remains of the branch line to Alston can be seen in the background. *Geoff Dowling*

Above: No 40.126 strains to accelerate a heavy stone train away from Peak Forest on 25 June 1976. *L. Peter Gater*

Left: No 40.069, the Class '40' which had a few inches of bodyside skirt removed during the 1960s in order that oil drainage pipes could be positioned externally, heads a northbound steel train through Wigan North Western on 26 June 1978. *David A. Flitcroft*

Right: No 40.068 climbs out of Arpley Yard onto the West Coast main line at Warrington with a train of empty hoppers on 26 May 1983. *Graham Scott-Lowe*

Below: No 40.044 pauses for a crew change at Warrington Bank Quay station while working a southbound oil train on 8 February 1977. No 40.188 is stabled in the up bay. *Bert Wynn*

Far left: No 40.120 awaits departure from Derby with the 'Gwent Valley Invader' railtour from Crewe to South Wales on 11 March 1978. *C. John Tuffs*

Above: No 40.026 arrives at Llandudno Junction with a Manchester-Holyhead train on 28 June 1978. The windscreen had been damaged en route, and the locomotive was removed before the train proceeded on its journey. *David A. Flitcroft*

Left: No 40.078, and a Class '08' diesel shunter, stabled at Perth station in August 1981. *Mike Esau*

Far left: No 40.058 passes under Harford Viaduct, near Norwich, with the summer Saturday 14.34 Yarmouth-Manchester Piccadilly on 3 September 1983.
David C. Pearce

Above: No 40.038 pilots BRCW Class '26/1' No 26.034 on the late-running 09.35 Glasgow Queen Street-Aberdeen near Cove Bay on 5 March 1979.
Brian Morrison

Left: During 1979, following the collapse of Penmanshiel Tunnel, some East Coast main line freight traffic was diverted over the Settle and Carlisle route. Here a class '40' emerges from the north end of Crosby Garrett Tunnel with one of the special freights, on 13 May 1979. *Chris Davis*

Above: No 40.158 crosses the River Tay at Perth with the 10.40 Perth-Aberdeen on 28 August 1981. *Mike Esau*

Left: No 40.131 crosses the Weaver Viaduct at Frodsham, Cheshire, with a southbound mixed freight in March 1983. This locomotive was one of the examples from which train heating boilers and the associated underslung water tanks were removed during the class's final years, as can be clearly seen in this view. *John Whitehouse*

Above right: No 40.068 heads a Monkton-Northwich coal train over the Huddersfield Canal near Bradley Wood Junction, west of Mirfield, in May 1983. *Roger Kaye*

Right: In pouring rain, No 40.086 heads the 16.30 Scunthorpe West Yard-Belmont ferrywagon train across Keadby swingbridge, near Althorpe, Yorkshire, on 14 April 1983. *Michael J. Collins*

Above: No 40.029 (formerly *Saxonia*) heads an eastbound oil train through Wakefield Kirkgate station, in damp and gloomy conditions on 21 February 1977. *Chris Davis*

Left: Green-liveried 40.122/D200 at the head of the 10.40 service for Leeds via the Settle and Carlisle route, at Carlisle station on 5 September 1983. *Graham Scott-Lowe*

Above right: No 40.050 awaits the right-away at Cyffordd Llandudno (Llandudno Junction) with the 11.57 Bangor-Manchester on 29 September 1982. *Peter Shoesmith*

Right: During heavy rain, No 40.015 (formerly *Aquitania*) stands in York station in the early hours of 25 April 1981 with a southbound parcels train. *Geoff Dowling*

Above: No 40.090, together with BR/Sulzer Class '25/2' No 25.135, stabled alongside Blackburn station on Sunday 16 May 1982.   *Tom Heavyside*

Below: No 40.178 heads a down train of ballast empties through Colwyn Bay station in the summer haze of 27 August 1980.   *A. Wyn Hobson*

Above: No 40.085 heads the 20.08(SX) Mossend Yard-Harwich Parkeston Quay freight through Bury St Edmunds station on 23 October 1982. *John C. Baker*

Right: No 40.168 heads a Dundee-Coatbridge freightliner train through Stirling station on 25 March 1981. *Michael Rhodes*

Left: No 40.082 passes
Normanton with a train of coal
containers bound for Healey Mills
on 6 April 1983.
Michael J. Collins

Below left: No 40.069 passes East
Usk, Monmouthshire, with the
05.50 Carlisle Kingmoor-Severn
Tunnel Junction freight on 25
March 1983. *Michael Rhodes*

Right: No 40.162 near Great Rocks
Junction, Peak Forest, on 8
August 1982. Unusually at this
date, this locomotive still
displayed four zeros in its
headcode panels. *C. John Tuffs*

Below: No 40.024 (formerly
Lucania) approaches Normanton
with a westbound oil train on 6
April 1983. Of interest is the signal
post on the left, carrying both
semaphore and colour-light
signals. *Michael J. Collins*

Left: 40.141 and 40.124 stabled at Northwich stabling point – the former steam shed adapted for modern use – on 25 March 1983. *Geoff Dowling*

Above: No 40.060, stabled in the old steam shed at Workington for minor repairs on 5 July 1983. This locomotive was a former Scottish Region example, rebuilt in 1965 with central headcode panels in place of its original connecting doors and headcode discs. *Michael Rhodes*

Right: No 40.007 at Haymarket depot, Edinburgh, on 14 August 1982. *C. John Tuffs*

Above: No 40.177 in the service area at the modern diesel maintenance depot at Tinsley, Sheffield, on 14 October 1979. *L. Peter Gater*

Left: No 40.069 at Inverness depot on 15 May 1982. *Cyril Lofthus*

Above right: 40.084 and 40.086 at Willesden diesel and electric depot, at the south end of the West Coast main line, after working the Class 40 Preservation Society's 'Silver Jubilee' railtour on 5 March 1983. *Graham Scott-Lowe*

Right: Nos 40.098 and 40.145 stabled at Buxton depot on 22 August 1979. *Geoff Pinder*

Above left: No 40.007 runs over
the Up Yard hump at Toton on 6
April 1978. *David C. Pearce*

Left: No 40.168 passes
Dringhouses Yard, York, with a
Teesside-Clitheroe cement train
on 7 April 1983.
Michael J. Collins

Above: No 40.058 shunts at
Beighton Permanent Way Depot,
south east of Sheffield, on 11
March 1979. *David Percival*

Right: No 40.057 waits to leave
Portobello Freightliner Terminal,
Edinburgh, with the 19.30 service
for Kings Cross on 16 June 1983.
Bert Wynn

Above left: No 40.083 climbs away from Manchester Victoria station with a through freight on 5 December 1982. *Ian McDonald*

Below left: No 40.087 heads a westbound mixed freight through Guide Bridge station on 12 June 1979. *Kevin Lane*

Above: No 40.029 (formerly *Saxonia*) heads a refuse container train from Manchester through Bolton station on 26 April 1982. *John Whitehouse*

Below: After arrival with a chartered excursion, No 40.024 (formerly *Lucania*) awaits a clear road into Chester depot on 15 October 1983. *A. Wyn Hobson*

Left: No 40.101 runs an unfitted freight from the Decoy Yards through the down centre road at Doncaster station on 20 May 1981. *Antony Guppy*

Above: No 40.061 emerges from the mist at New Mills South Junction with the summer Saturday 08.18 Manchester Piccadilly-Skegness in August 1982. *Geoff Dowling*

Below: On a bitterly cold, foggy day in February 1980, No 40.081 and Class '47/0' No 47.290 meet with freights at Barrow Hill, near Chesterfield. *Roger Kaye*

Left: A glimpse of No 40.079 at Disley, on the Stockport-Buxton line, on 18 September 1983. *Steve Turner*

Above: No 40.047 noses under the town walls at Conwy with a train of heavy stone blocks from Penmaenmawr Granite Works, for sea-defence work on the North Wales coast, on 2 July 1983. *Geoff Dowling*

Right: No 40.063 hauls two HAA hopper wagons towards Edinburgh Waverley station on 31 August 1982. *C. John Tuffs*

Left: No 40.004 skirts the River Usk near Caerleon, Monmouthshire, with a special Basford Hall-Severn Tunnel Junction mineral train on 5 August 1983. *Michael Rhodes*

Below left: A Class '40' heads a Saturday Edinburgh-Newcastle extra across the Royal Border Viaduct at Berwick-upon-Tweed on 28 June 1980. *Michael Rhodes*

Above: No 40.082 heads the 17.14 Workington-Dover Town freight across Eskmeals Viaduct, near Sellafield, on the Cumbrian coast, on 13 July 1983. *Kim Fullbrook*

Below: No 40.060 runs down along the coast at Parton, Cumbria, towards Corkickle, where it will pick up a freight for Ince, in Lancashire, on 5 July 1983. *Michael Rhodes*

Above: Two machines of superseded design at March on 1 May 1982: an old fuel pump, and Class '40' No 40.012 (formerly named *Aureol*) preparing to depart for Peterborough and the Nene Valley Railway with the 'Anglian Whistler' railtour. *David C. Pearce*